The Last
Frontier

God's Expectations of You before the Appearing of Jesus

THE LAST FRONTIER

ISBN 0-9655352-9-0
Unless otherwise stated, all Scripture
quotations are taken from
The *King James Version* of the Bible.

Jerry Savelle Ministries International
P.O. Box 748
Crowley, TX 76036
(817) 297-3155
Website: www.jsmi.org

TABLE OF CONTENTS

INTRODUCTION
The Last Frontier

What I'm about to share with you could change the course of your life forever. If there are things in your life that you've been believing God for, perhaps for many years, and still haven't seen the manifestation of them, then this could be the answer to your breakthrough.

I believe the appearing of Jesus is so close, and we don't have very much time left on this earth. However, there are many things left for us to do, and we have to be equipped to do them. God is expecting us to be in the best spiritual shape of our lives. Why? Because this is the *Last Frontier.*

One of the definitions that *Webster's Dictionary* gives for the word ***frontier*** is *a new or unexplored area of thought or knowledge.*

What you are about to read may be new or unexplored knowledge. For some, it might be knowledge that needs to be rekindled. Regardless, I personally believe that it is the *last frontier* before the appearing of the Lord!

God began to deal with me about the subject of this book back in 1994. I had a visitation of the Lord for several days in a row. I didn't see Him, but I knew His presence was there. After He shared this message with me, it seemed that everywhere I preached it, the people were not ready to hear it. I literally had to put it on the shelf until the proper time.

But now God has said, "It's time for you to preach this everywhere you go. They will receive it. If they won't, then they'll not experience My best."

So I'm under obligation. I have a divine mandate to share this message with you. I believe that you are ready, and I believe it will have a profound impact upon your life just as it has on mine.

I want to encourage you to read this book with an open heart and allow the words on these pages to drop into your spirit and help you to grasp God's plan for your life. It is a very timely and life-changing message. It's God's expectation of YOU before the appearing of Jesus.

CHAPTER 1

Training for the Gold

1

Training for the Gold

In 1984, Carolyn and I had the privilege of attending the Olympic Games in Los Angeles, California. We went to the Track and Field Events, Gymnastics, and, of course, Boxing. We had so much fun watching those athletes who had trained for years for that one moment. I enjoy watching people excel in what they do.

To those trained athletes, the Gold Medal represents the best or the ultimate reward for all their hard work. To be in competition for the Gold Medal, you must be highly disciplined, committed, dedicated, willing to do things that other people are not willing to do, and have a no-quit attitude. You make rules on yourself, you draw boundaries around yourself, and you simply do not compromise . . . if you're aiming for the Gold!

I've never heard any Olympian say, "I'm training for the Bronze." That's not the way a potential Gold Medallist thinks. He doesn't ask the coach, "What's the least amount of laps I have to run just to get into the game?"

"Can I eat anything I want and still get in the game?"

No.

"Can I stay out all night running around, getting no rest and still make it to the game?"

No.

To even be eligible to train for the Olympics, they have to go all out, so-to-speak, to attain their goal. Winning the Silver or Bronze Medal is nothing to scoff at, but it doesn't represent the best.

In comparison, it appears that most Christians want what other successful, prosperous, and extremely blessed Christians have, but they're not willing to do what they did to get there. You can't expect the rewards of diligence if you refuse to become diligent.

You can't decide that you want to be in the Olympics two weeks before they start. You're not in shape. You haven't trained. You're not disciplined. Your mind hasn't been renewed to that of an Olympian. I'm sorry, but the coach is not going to choose you. You're not prepared.

It's the same way with God. You may have a desire for God's best, but it takes a life of discipline to acquire it. Are you living a disciplined lifestyle? Are you living a life that is pleasing to God? If not, then you're not prepared. And, I'm sorry, but God is not going to choose you to pour His blessings upon. He wants to, but you must meet His requirements.

God expects displine, commitment, focus and faithfulness from us to win the Gold (or God's best).

Aim for the Finish Line

1 Corinthians 9:26 in the Message translation says, *I don't know about you, but I'm running hard for the finish line. I'm giving it everything I've got. No sloppy living for me!*

You can't expect the Gold if you're going to be sloppy spiritually. It takes discipline. For the most part, *discipline* is not a favorite word in Charismatic circles. When I talk about discipline, I've had people say, "That's bondage, Brother." No, it's not bondage. It's what produces God's best in your life. But what is God's best?

Back when I first surrendered my life to the Lord and was absorbing everything I could about the Word of faith from Kenneth Copeland, I heard him make a statement that changed my thinking drastically.

He said, "Most of you think that the nature of God is miraculous, but it's not."

And he just paused for a moment.

I was sitting there thinking to myself, *You could have fooled me! I thought it was. When I think of God, I think of miracles.*

Then he repeated it, "Most of you think that the nature of God is miraculous, but it's not."

He said, "The nature of God is abundance. Miracles only happen when there's lack."

What a statement! The only time you need a miracle is when there's lack. A lack of what? A lack of abundance. We've been satisfied with living from financial miracle to financial miracle, but that's not God's best.

His best is for us to have more than enough. If we're truly walking in the abundance that God has prepared for us, then we are so blessed that we don't need a miracle.

Now don't misunderstand me. I'm not saying that I have arrived at this place yet. What I'm saying is, let's set our sights higher. Let's go for the Gold. That's what I'm doing—I'm going for God's best!

What is the *Gold?*

Going for the Gold, or God's best, is more than being blessed occasionally. It means walking in the blessings of God every day of your life. We should be exactly what the Word says: Blessed coming in, going out, in the city, in the field, and in everything we set our hands to do. (Deuteronomy 28:3).

It seems that most Christians are satisfied with whatever is lower than Bronze. "We're going for 'the Copper'! And we hope to get 'Tinfoil'!"

Apparently, the Body of Christ is just satisfied with whatever they can get. But God is saying, "Go for the Gold!" I'm not talking about just financially but in every area of our lives.

God's best is for us to be blessed. Let that sink in for a moment. Do you really understand the true meaning of *blessed?*

Blessed means that you have entered into a state of being. You could say that people who are blessed are experiencing God's best. They are now able to be a blessing to others.

God wants you so blessed that you have to give some of it away.

God wants you so blessed that you can be the answer to someone else's prayer.

God wants you so blessed that you can meet the needs of others and never even miss what you gave away.

You might be saying, "But I'm not living like that." Keep standing. God intended for you and me, as the seed of Abraham, to be blessed every day of our lives. If you'll demand discipline, obedience and faithfulness in your life, then it's just a matter of time and you'll arrive at this place.

If you had a choice to live in divine health or be healed every six weeks, which would you choose? Divine health. When God looks at you, He does not see you as the sick trying to get healed. He sees you as the healed defending your right to stay well. God's looking through the Blood of Jesus. God is looking through that Sacrifice at Calvary. If God agrees with you that you're sick, then He has to deny the Blood. He would have to deny those stripes on Jesus' back.

For the most part, many of God's people have not lived in health so they need healing frequently. Most of God's people have not lived in divine prosperity so they constantly need financial miracles. It's time to set our sights higher. Let's set our sights on divine health, divine prosperity, and living extremely blessed every day of our lives.

God wants us blessed so that we can be a blessing. I define the word ***blessing*** as *an instrument through which God's divine favor flows, bringing joy, happiness and prosperity, and preventing misfortune in the lives of others.* That's God's best.

If you don't have a revelation of God's will for you to be blessed, then you'll never experience His best for your life.

Let's find out what God's intention was for mankind from the very beginning.

And God said, Let us make man in our image, after our likeness: and let them have dominion over the fish of the sea, and over the fowl of the air, and over the cattle, and over all the earth, and over every creeping thing that creepeth upon the earth.

So God created man in his own image, in the image of God created he him; male and female created he them.

And God blessed them . . .

Genesis 1:26-28

The Scriptural definition for **blessed** is to become *the object of God's favor* and *empowered to prosper.* Many people have a hard time believing that God loves them that much. God didn't make man so He'd have something to put on the earth. He made earth as a gift to man. Everything God has ever made was made with you and me in mind.

Perhaps you need to get a revelation of just how special you are to God. Peter says, "We are a peculiar people." In the literal Greek, that means a *special treasure.* You are God's special treasure.

In fact, the Apostle Paul prayed that we would understand the breadth, the length, the depth, and the height of the love of God (Ephesians 3:18). There are still depths of God's love that we haven't fully grasped yet.

God is saying, "You are the object of My favor, and it is My best for you to be empowered to prosper in every area of your life." In other words, you have the potential to be a Gold Medallist. You can have God's best.

Now that should make you feel very special. Not only that, but it also should cause you to get up in the morning with a dance in your step, your head held up high, and no matter what you're going through, you just say to the devil, "It's not over yet. I'm the object of God's favor, and before the day is up, I will be victorious!"

Which End Are You On?

Carolyn and I have come a long way since 1969 when we first learned that God wanted us blessed. We were the ones needing divine intervention every hour of the day. We were on the receiving end believing God for everything.

When we first started out, we would go to meetings to hear Kenneth Copeland or Kenneth Hagin, and we would drive a couple hundred miles to get there. It would take every dime we had just to put gasoline in the car. We couldn't afford a hotel room, and so we'd stay in the car and eat peanut butter and jelly sandwiches.

After the meeting, somebody might say, "Would you like to go out and eat?" We would have to decline the invitation because we didn't know if they were buying, and we couldn't take the chance because we didn't have any money.

We would go back to our car, take out our peanut butter sandwiches, and have lunch. We were so happy to be there listening to the Word because we knew that what these men were preaching was about to take us from Egypt to Canaan land, praise God.

We knew that our days of eating peanut butter sandwiches in the car were coming to an end. It wouldn't be long, and we would not only be feeding ourselves but feeding other people as well. We knew that God would bless us if we would dare believe for it, aim for it, and go for the Gold.

Today, I love buying meals for other people. I even do it for total strangers. Many times I'll go to a restaurant just looking for somebody to buy a meal for. Why? Because I remember when.

Another thing I love to do is provide people with a hotel room. Why? Because there was a time when we couldn't stay in a hotel room. We would spend the night in the car in the church parking lot. You know, it's not really that bad. The next morning, you get good seats! You're the first ones there!

But we haven't had to sleep in the car in a long, long time. We haven't had to eat peanut butter sandwiches in the car in a long, long time. If I happen to walk through the parking lot and see somebody doing that, I'm going to bless them. That tells me they're hungry for God. I know where God brought me, and He's going to take them there if they will dare believe for it and go for the Gold.

It's much more fun being on the giving end. In order to be on the giving end, you have to be blessed. Don't get me wrong. I love receiving, but being able to give is so much fun.

God's plan for His people to be blessed is expressed throughout the Bible from one generation to another. It continued through Noah, Abraham, Isaac, and Jacob, and now to us because we are the seed of Abraham.

*And Abraham was old, and well stricken in age: and **the Lord had blessed Abraham in all things**.*

Genesis 24:1

I had a preacher say to me one time, "Oh, Brother Jerry, that was only spiritual blessings. That's what God was talking about."

Then somebody needs to tell God. Because His Word says, "all things." If you study the life of

Abraham, you'll find out that the blessings included wealth, cattle, land, and material things. God blessed him in all things. Of course, God wants us blessed spiritually, but it doesn't end there. He wants us blessed in every area of our lives.

According to Genesis 25:11, God's blessings didn't stop with Abraham. They continued with Abraham's seed just as God had promised. And this includes you and me!

So how do we experience the blessings of Abraham? First, we must get our lives in line with the Word of God. We must discipline ourselves in every area. Going for the Gold means that we can't be like the average Christian.

Become a Barrier Breaker

Know ye not that they which run in a race run all, but one receiveth the prize? So run, that ye may obtain.

And every man that striveth for the mastery is temperate in all things. Now they do it to obtain a corruptible crown; but we an incorruptible.

I therefore so run, not as uncertainly; so fight I, not as one that beateth the air:

But I keep under my body, and bring it into subjection: lest that by any means, when I have preached to others, I myself should be a castaway.

1 Corinthians 9:24-27

Verse 25, in the Amplified says, *Now every athlete who goes into training conducts himself temperately and restricts himself in all things.*

The person who is serious about winning the Gold restricts himself in all things. You cannot expect mediocre training to produce Gold Medal results. That's not how it works.

Average athletes don't win Gold Medals. Average athletes don't go to the Super Bowl. Average Christians don't abound in blessings. It's those who excel. It's those who will do not only what is required but they also go beyond. It's those who refuse to quit until they have attained God's best.

Don't stop reading. Now you're going to find out exactly what's been holding you back, how to remove it, and how to move into God's best for your life!

CHAPTER 2

What's Stopping Your Breakthrough?

2

What's Stopping Your Breakthrough?

When I first surrendered my life to preach, I witnessed God's supernatural power in the lives of people almost immediately. I was thrust into a supernatural ministry almost from day one even before I went to work for Brother Kenneth Copeland. I've seen times when the power of God would just absolutely roll into a place like waves on the ocean, and you couldn't preach anymore because people were being set free right before your eyes.

I've had the privilege of watching God's power demonstrated in marvelous ways. But recently, I began asking, "Father, why are we not seeing more of this? Why aren't we seeing Your power in demonstration in a greater way?" It's not God's best that we see less of His glory in these last days preceding the appearing of Jesus. We should be seeing more! That's when He led me into this study.

Is there something in your life that has taken too long to manifest and you've wondered why? Could it be something that you're doing, or perhaps not doing, that is prolonging the answer to your prayers? Let's take a look at some things that the Holy Spirit revealed to me. Perhaps they will be the answer you've been looking for.

Three Reasons for Not Enjoying God's Best

What's stopping your breakthrough from manifesting?

1. <u>A Lack of Knowledge</u>.

My people are destroyed for lack of knowledge.

Hosea 4:6

You can't enjoy something that you don't even know exists. Do you remember the first time you discovered, "By His stripes we are healed"? Did that change the way you lived? Or what about the day you found out that you have authority as a believer? Did that change your life?

I'll never forget the day I read Brother Kenneth Hagin's book back in 1969 entitled, *Right and Wrong Thinking.* What a revelation! It transformed my thinking about everything.

I didn't see an immediate outward change as far as my financial situation was concerned; I still had the same problems as I did before I read the book, but my perspective about them changed!

Carolyn and I began acting on everything we read and heard, and things started changing. With God, it's not *if* it happens, it's *when* it happens. If you stick to it, then it's just a matter of time.

Prior to us listening to those tapes by Kenneth Copeland and reading books by Kenneth Hagin, we had no knowledge of God's will for our lives. We didn't know we had a right to live in health. We didn't know we had a right to be blessed. We didn't know that God would take care of us financially. Our lack of knowledge was keeping us from enjoying something that God had already pre-planned for us to have.

But once we began to gain knowledge, then we began to pursue what God said belonged to us, and it began to happen.

This book of the law shall not depart out of thy mouth; but thou shalt meditate therein day and night, that thou mayest observe to do according to all that is written therein: for then thou shalt make thy way prosperous, and then thou shalt have good success.

Joshua 1:8

In order to gain knowledge, you have to meditate the Word of God day and night. You have to discover exactly who you are and what you are entitled to as a child of God. Your knowledge will increase, and you'll begin walking in the revelations that you've received.

So then faith cometh by hearing, and hearing by the word of God.

Romans 10:17

Your faith will develop and grow according to the amount of God's Word that you deposit into your spirit. Your knowledge will increase and so will your blessings. You'll begin to enjoy God's best as never before.

2. <u>A failure to correctly appropriate the laws of faith</u>.

Did you know that there are laws that govern faith? The Bible says that God knows your needs even before you ask. But according to James 4:2, He still requires that we ask.

Ye lust, and have not: ye kill, and desire to have, and cannot obtain: ye fight and war, yet <u>ye have not, because ye ask not.</u>

Asking, you could say, is the first step to appropriating the law of faith. God requires that we <u>ask</u>.

Verse three continues to say, *Ye ask, and receive not, because <u>ye ask amiss</u> . . .*

In other words, even though you're asking, you could be asking improperly or with wrong motives.

Jesus said, *If ye shall ask any thing in my name, I will do it* (John 14:14).

The Bible also says, *Ask, and it shall be given you; seek, and ye shall find; knock, and it shall be opened unto you* (Matthew 7:7). So what does asking amiss mean? Let's find out and see if it applies to you.

And Jesus answering saith unto them, Have faith in God.

For verily I say unto you, That whosoever shall say unto this mountain, Be thou removed, and be thou cast into the sea; and shall not doubt in his heart, but shall believe that those things which he saith shall come to pass; he shall have whatsoever he saith.

Therefore I say unto you, What things soever ye desire, when ye pray, believe that ye receive them, and ye shall have them.

Mark 11:22-24

One example of asking amiss is found in this verse. If you prayed, but you didn't believe you received when you prayed, then you are really doubting God's ability to perform His Word, with signs following, in your life. That's asking amiss.

"Well, we're just hoping and praying, but you never know what God's going to do."

Wait a minute. Didn't you just pray? Then why didn't you believe that He would do it?

If you wait until you see the results before you believe, then it's highly unlikely that you'll ever have victory in your prayer life. Jesus indicated in His teachings that if you have to see it or feel it first, then that's being "faithless."

Verse 25 reveals another way we ask amiss. *And when ye stand praying, **forgive**, if ye have aught against any: that your Father also which is in heaven may forgive you your trespasses.*

You may be saying all the right things: "I'm more than a conqueror. I'm a world overcomer. My God supplies all my needs. I believe I receive when I pray," and then somebody says to you, "How's your wife?"

"Well, she and I don't get along. She really hurt me, and I'll never forgive her for it."

Then you've asked amiss.

You've got aught against someone. That violates the law of faith. You can confess all the right things, you can even believe you received when you prayed, but if you've got aught in your heart against someone, then you've asked amiss. They are now controlling your prayer life and your destiny.

You have to forgive.

Is hanging onto that unforgiveness worth being robbed of God's best? No. Then why not let go of it?

Many years ago, I had a partner whose wife was dying of cancer. He called and asked me if I would go to the hospital and pray for her. I said I'd be happy to.

As I was flying to their city, the Lord told me, "Son, it's not My will that she die. But she will . . . if she doesn't forgive her husband. Satan will kill her if she doesn't forgive her husband. Go tell her that."

I said, "Lord, I don't want to tell her that. You tell her!"

He said, "I will . . . through you."

I didn't want to get into their personal affairs. Then, I thought, *What if I'm wrong? What if this is just some thought I had?* But I knew it was God. I just didn't want to do it.

I went to the hospital, and she was lying there dying of cancer. I walked over to her, and I said, "This is hard for me to do, but I have to obey God. The Spirit of God spoke to me and told me that it's not His will that you die. He will deliver you from this cancer. You'll get up out of this bed and walk away free if you'll do what God's telling you."

Then I said, "I don't want to know what it's about. You don't have to tell me anything, but I do know something happened in your marriage, and you've never forgiven your husband for it. And if you don't forgive him, then you've given the devil a foothold, and he's going to kill you. If you'll forgive your husband, God will deliver you."

She looked up at me and said, "I will never forgive him." She went on to say, "I'll go to my grave with this."

Well, not long after that, they buried her. And these were "faith people"!

"I don't understand, Brother Jerry. Why did she die? They were tithers, they were givers, and they confessed all the right Scriptures. Why did she die?"

She didn't correctly appropriate the law of faith which includes, "And when ye pray, forgive." She didn't forgive.

I'm totally convinced that situation grieved the heart of God. It wasn't His will. But He's not going to violate His own Word.

I encourage you right now, this very minute, to say, "God, I forgive. I release any and all offenses that have come against me. I let it go. I am not going to allow unforgiveness or aught against anyone to hinder my prayer life or control my destiny. I forgive that person. I forgive those people. I release them in Jesus' name."

Now give the Lord a shout of praise. Don't carry that junk around with you. That's excess baggage. Those are weights. You can't run this race with all those weights on you. Let them go once and for all.

3. <u>No revelation of the fear of the Lord.</u>

A few years ago while hosting our annual Revival Fires Conference, Gloria Copeland was one of our guest speakers. During her session, she made a statement that I have never forgotten. She said, "They've called us *Word* people, and they've called us *Faith* people. But nobody's ever called us *Holy* people."

Now in order for you to receive what I have to say to you by the Spirit of God, you're going to have to put all the religious preconceptions you may have had about *holiness* on the shelf for a moment. Don't put up a wall right now. Open your heart and receive what the Lord has given me because it will change your life forever.

So many of God's people today have no insight whatsoever as to what it means to walk in the fear of the Lord. I call it the *Last Frontier.* It should have been the first thing we learned as believers, but it looks as though it's going to be the last.

A Spirit of Fear vs. the Fear of the Lord

The fear of the Lord is not to be confused with a spirit of fear. Many times, that's why people put up walls when they even hear the phrase, *the fear of the Lord.*

The fear of the Lord is not referring to being afraid of God. We're talking about reverence for God. We're talking about worshiping God and being amazed at His greatness. We're talking about being in awe of His magnificence. But it also means not wanting to do anything that would displease Him because you love Him so much. It doesn't mean pleasing Him just because you're afraid He might kill you if you don't.

Somebody may say, "Doesn't the Bible talk about the wrath of God?"

Yes, it does. But you will never see it. You're His child. There will be people who reject Jesus and will find out that there is a side of God called wrath, but you and I will never witness the wrath of God.

I would never do anything to harm my own children. They've done things that have displeased me, but it certainly didn't change my love for them. I still loved them just the same. I didn't start trying to figure out a way I could harm them. Well, God is no different with His children.

In the Old Testament, they saw the wrath of God from time to time because they weren't born again people. The Blood of Jesus hadn't been shed at that point. God told them, "If you obey, these blessings will come on you. If you don't, these curses will come on you." It wasn't enjoyable to Him for those curses to come on His people. It broke His heart because that wasn't His best. But, He was obligated to His own Word. He's a Sovereign God.

A simple definition of *holiness* is: **you love what God loves and you hate what God hates.** To walk in the fear of the Lord simply means you don't want to do anything to displease Him. You don't want to do anything that you think might dishonor Him.

Most of the teaching I've heard over the years on the fear of the Lord was condemning. But a true revelation of the fear of the Lord will not condemn you; it will set you free.

The Fear of the Lord Is . . .

If you've ever wondered what the fear of the Lord is, then look at Proverbs 8:13: *The fear of the Lord is to hate evil. . .* That's it.

The Amplified Bible says, *The reverent fear and worshipful awe of the Lord [includes] the hatred of evil.*

It continues to say, *The fear of the Lord is to hate evil: pride, and arrogancy, and the evil way, and the froward mouth, do I hate.*

There's nothing difficult about that. There's nothing religious about that. It's just simply *hating evil.* You could say that the fear of the Lord and holiness are synonymous. It's loving what God loves and hating what God hates.

Well, let's define what *evil* is and see if we truly hate it. *W. E. Vine's* defines the word **evil** as *things that are bad, contemptible, wicked, harmful, wrong, and worthless.* *Webster's Dictionary* defines **evil** as *that which is morally bad or morally wrong.*

The word **hate** simply means *to despise, to greatly dislike, to have no tolerance for.*

Now let's inject these definitions into this Scripture and see how it comes out. **The fear of the Lord is to despise, to greatly dislike, and to have no tolerance for things that are bad, contemptible, wicked, harmful, wrong and worthless.**

Now let's inject *Webster's* definition into the verse: **The fear of the Lord is to despise, to dislike greatly, to have no tolerance for anything that is morally bad or morally wrong.**

Does that describe the way most of the Body of Christ lives? No. We have become desensitized to what is morally wrong.

Have you ever been told at some time in your life, "Let your conscience be your guide?" Where do you think that came from? The Bible.

"Well, Brother Jerry, I didn't know that what I was doing was wrong."

Yes, you did! Your conscience warned you. That inward witness warned you. You have to go against what the Spirit of God is saying to you to engage in things that are morally wrong.

There was a person I had to minister to about some morally wrong decisions he had made in his life, and I said, "You did wrong. You knew it when you went into it, and you had to be willing to do it to allow it to happen."

And the person said, "Well, are you going to condemn me over this?"

I said, "No. I'm not. But it's time for you to crucify your flesh, then you're not going to be doing these things that God considers morally wrong."

Doesn't the Bible tell us we are to consider ourselves as dead to sin, and alive unto righteousness (Romans 6:11)?

So for you to do something that is morally wrong, then you had to raise that old dead man. You had to raise that old dead man in order to get involved in something that you know displeases God. You had to go against your true nature. Your nature is the nature of God.

To continually engage in things that are morally wrong means that either there was no revelation of the fear of the Lord or no willingness to walk in that revelation. When you find yourself in a situation that is questionable, then just ask yourself, "Does God hate this?" And if you're not sure, then go read your Bible.

The word **hate** is also defined as *to regard with extreme aversion, to have great dislike for, to detest, and unwilling to tolerate.*

If you're not at the place where you detest hearing God's name used in vain, then you've become desensitized. The world thinks you can't make a movie without using God's name in vain in every other sentence. They think you can't make a movie without using four-letter words that you hope your children never hear. They think you can't make a movie without nudity. And if we get to the point where we're so desperate for entertainment that we become desensitized to watching something that God hates, then we simply don't hate evil anymore. We've become tolerant.

We should be unwilling to tolerate anything that displeases the One who gave His life for us. That's not hard. Walking in the fear of the Lord is not hard, and it's not bondage. It's just a matter of choice.

I'm not trying to put anybody down or condemn anyone, but at the same time, I'm not going to whitewash the Word of God. I've got to speak the truth. I'm not telling you to do something that I haven't had to put into practice in my own life.

What will walking in the fear of the Lord produce?

The fear of the Lord tendeth to life: and he that hath it (this revelation of the fear of the Lord) *shall abide satisfied; he shall not be visited with evil.*

Proverbs 19:23

The Amplified says, *The reverent, worshipful fear of the Lord leads to life.*

What kind of life? The abounding, abundant, overflowing, and blessed life. The Bible says the fear of the Lord is the beginning of knowledge (Proverbs 1:7). In other words, you have to have a revelation of this if you are truly going to walk in the knowledge of God. A revelation of walking in the fear of the Lord will lead you to the Gold— God's best!

How Would You Describe Your Life?

Hating evil. Does that describe your life? Does that describe how you feel? Do you hate what God hates? Can you go to places that God would consider evil, and it not grieve your spirit? Can you listen to things that God considers evil and not sense that you're displeasing Him? Can you watch things that God would consider evil and not be convicted by it? If so, then you've become desensitized.

However, there's hope. All of us have been guilty of this in one way or another. But God is saying all you've got to do is repent. Return to your first love (Revelation 2:4-5). In other words, turn around. Make an about face. Stir yourself up. There is hope.

But we can't take this lightly.

By mercy and truth iniquity is purged.

Proverbs 16:6

When we hear the truth, and we're willing to receive it, then God provides the mercy and the grace. God says, "Yes, you've been wrong. Yes, you've not pleased Me in some areas of your life. However, you've heard the truth, you've received the truth, and you've yielded to the truth, now receive My mercy." (Author's paraphrase.)

God doesn't condemn you. He says, "Now, receive My mercy. Pick yourself up. Brush yourself off. And now get on the right course."

When you have a true revelation of the fear of the Lord, you are not going to allow yourself to be desensitized to things that God considers evil. You will depart from it. You will remove yourself from it.

Psalm 15:1-2 asks this question: *Lord, who shall abide in thy tabernacle? who shall dwell in thy holy hill?*

Verse 2 (Amplified) says, *He who walks and lives uprightly and blamelessly.*

That's another key to living a blessed life . . . to live uprightly. God wants you to live a holy life. He wants you to hate what He hates and love what He loves.

Find the Treasure

The Lord is exalted; for he dwelleth on high: he hath filled Zion with judgment and righteousness.

*And wisdom and knowledge shall be the stability of thy times, and strength of salvation: **the fear of the Lord** is his treasure.*

Isaiah 33:5-6

The Bible tells us that there is a treasure to be found only by having a revelation of the fear of the Lord. What is that treasure?

He hath made the earth by his power, he hath established the world by his wisdom, and hath stretched out the heavens by his discretion.

When he uttereth his voice, there is a multitude of waters in the heavens, and he causeth the vapours to ascend from the ends of the earth; he maketh lightnings with rain, and bringeth forth the wind out of his treasures.

Jeremiah 10:12-13

This treasure is where all of God's power emanates from. This treasure is where the signs and the wonders come from. This treasure is where the supernatural resides.

When we begin to walk in the fear of the Lord, then we'll begin to witness the glory of God in our lives as never before.

That's where God's leading us! He said, "The glory of the latter church shall be greater than the glory of the former church" (Haggai 2:9). We will never see the greater glory without a revelation of this and the application of it in our lives. I'm going for that treasure! And I hope you'll go with me. That's where our breakthrough is.

Don't allow anything to stop you from receiving the breakthrough you've been believing God for. Continue to meditate the Word, feed your spirit man, correctly appropriate the laws of faith, release all unforgiveness and begin walking in the fear of the Lord. Now you're ready to begin to experience God's best.

CHAPTER 3

Take Inventory
of Your Life

3

Take Inventory of Your Life

Just for a moment, I encourage you to take an inventory of your present lifestyle. Are there things in your life that you know are not pleasing to God? Have you been involved in situations that grieved the Holy Spirit, yet you still went through with them? God is saying, "It's time to get rid of it." We can no longer have a tolerance for anything that God considers morally wrong.

You may be asking yourself, "How do I take inventory? Where do I begin?"

The Holy Guest

I'll tell you a real simple way to walk in a revelation of the fear of the Lord and how to take inventory of your life. A friend of mine shared with me that in some Old English writings the phrase *Holy Ghost* is translated *Holy Guest.* So, consider the Holy Ghost as your Holy Guest everywhere you go and in everything you do. Your Holy Guest is with you all the time. I like to refer to it as practicing the presence of the Holy Spirit.

Walking in that revelation will make you think twice about the activities you engage in as well as the words you speak, the things you watch, your conduct, your behavior . . . everything.

Before you go somewhere, before you read something, before you watch something, ask your Holy Guest if it will grieve Him. If you're about to go to a movie, and they're using God's name in vain, committing adultery, showing nudity and per-version, then simply ask your "Holy Guest" if He's comfortable with you going to see this.

Remember, we're training for the Gold. People who are training for the Gold don't do what everyone else does.

I consider Brother Oral Roberts to be my spiritual grandfather. I love and respect him greatly. Carolyn and I have had the privilege of having him and Evelyn in our home. Can you imagine me saying to him, "Brother Roberts, you're an honored guest in the Savelle home. After dinner, you and I will go into my study and watch television. Please overlook the nudity, the adultery, the perversion, the cussing and the using of God's name in vain. I'm sorry but it's the only thing that's on!"

Not for one minute would I subject a man like that, as my honored guest, to watch filth in my home. Well, there's Somebody in my home who's far greater. He's called the Holy Ghost. He is my Holy Guest. Can He watch what I'm watching? Can He read what I'm reading? Can He go where I go?

No Compromise

One of the things that attracted me to my wife, Carolyn, when we were dating was that she would not compromise. We grew up together on the same street, but it wasn't until I was in my second year of college and she was a senior in high school that we started dating. She loved God, and I was running from God.

When we were dating, she would not go to a place that she considered to be a sinful environment. She was totally dedicated to God, and she would not do anything that she thought would displease Him.

I had never dated a girl like her before. I didn't really want to be with her, but I couldn't stay away from her. If I was going to date Carolyn Creech, it was going to be at church. I had to go to youth rallies in order to be with her. I had to go to camp meetings and revivals to be with her. That was her standard, and she wouldn't change. That's what God is looking for in His people today—no compromise!

You're Responsible for What You Know

I sense God saying, "You've played church long enough. It's time to set your sights higher. It's time to go for the Gold."

I want you to notice what happens to those who refuse to walk in the fear of the Lord.

*Then shall they call upon me, but I will not answer; they shall seek me early, but they shall not find me: For that they hated knowledge, and **did not choose the fear of the Lord**: They would none of my counsel: they despised all my reproof.*

Proverbs 1:28-30

Did you see that? They asked, but they didn't get an answer. They sought God diligently, but they could not find Him. Why? Because they refused to walk in the fear of the Lord.

Up to now, we may have been able to get away with some things, but now that we know better, we are responsible for what we've seen in His Word.

If you want God's best in your life, if you want every prayer answered, and if you want the desires of your heart to be manifested, then you can no longer ignore this revelation.

*O fear the Lord, ye his saints: for **there is no want to them that fear him**.*

Psalm 34:9

That sounds like God's best. Wouldn't you say "no want" is God's best?

Psalm 112:1 says, *Praise ye the Lord. Blessed is the man that feareth the Lord . . .* The Amplified says *. . . Blessed (happy, fortunate, to be envied) is the man who fears (reveres and worships) the Lord, who delights greatly in His commandments.*

Verses two and three continue explaining what the person who walks in a revelation of the fear of the Lord will attain: *His seed shall be mighty upon the earth: the generation of the upright shall be blessed. Wealth and riches shall be in his house: and his righteousness endureth for ever.* Look what we can expect if we'll simply obey the Word of God.

What does the Word say about our conduct and behavior?

Blessed (happy, fortunate, to be envied) are the undefiled (the upright, truly sincere, and blameless) in the way [of the revealed will of God], who walk (order their conduct and conversation) in the law of the Lord (the whole of God's revealed will).

Psalm 119:1 (Amplified)

God says He will bless those who walk orderly in their conduct.

The reward of humility and the reverent and wor-shipful fear of the Lord is riches and honor and life.

Proverbs 22:4 (Amplified)

Remove the Unprofitable Things

The Apostle Paul wrote in 1 Corinthians 6:12, *All things are lawful unto me, but all things are not expedient.*

The word **expedient** means *profitable*. Paul is saying, "I've discovered that there are some things in my life that are not necessarily sinful, but they're just no longer profitable." (Author's paraphrase).

I began asking God to reveal to me anything in my life that was unprofitable. I'm willing to remove it. I'm willing to walk away from it. I'm willing to give it up. How about you?

It's not really a sacrifice when you fully under-stand that God rewards you when you're willing to get rid of the unprofitable things in your life!

If we are going to be used mightily in these last days, and if we are going to be the people that God pours His blessings on, then we've got to be sure that our lives are pure, and we are living upright and holy before God.

I personally believe that this is the revelation that is going to usher in the appearing of Jesus. It's the *last frontier* for the Body of Christ.

Invite the Holy Spirit to do an inventory in your life. Don't hide anything. Let Him in every clos-et; open every door. And when He says, "Now that's not profitable anymore," then immediately accept it. Don't feel like you're being robbed of something. God's leading you to the Gold.

If we are to obtain the Gold, then we must be willing to remove the unprofitable things in our lives. Unprofitable things can become weights, and weights can hinder our progression and slow us down.

Hebrews 12:1 says, . . . *let us lay aside every weight.*

The Amplified says, . . . *let us strip off and throw aside every encumbrance.*

The Message translation calls it *spiritual fat.*

You can't win the Gold if you're carrying around a lot of spiritual fat. It's time for strict training. Strict training demands strict discipline.

Put Restrictions on Yourself

Most people don't like restrictions. They want to eat what they want to eat, as much as they want to eat, watch what they want to watch, go where they want to go. And if some preacher starts telling them to bring some discipline into their lives, they start backstroking out of the church and find another one.

You cannot expect mediocre training to produce Gold Medal results. When those Olympic athletes make a decision to go for the Gold, they have to take a complete inventory of their present lifestyle and start making the necessary changes. They have to begin conditioning their bodies through vigorous exercise. They have to renew their thinking. They can't act like everyone else and expect to win the Gold. Well, neither can we.

If you're going for God's best, then you'll need to take inventory of your present lifestyle today. There may be things holding you back. Be willing to get rid of them. You'll find that it will be well worth it. God will reward you.

And may the Lord make you to increase and excel and overflow in love for one another.

1 Thessalonians 3:12 (Amplified)

God is saying, "I don't want you to be average at anything, not even where your love for one another is concerned. I want you to excel." (Author's paraphrase). God wants us to excel in every area of our lives so we can experience His best.

I discovered in my *Noah Webster 1828 Dictionary* that one of the definitions for the word *best* is *to excel, to surpass, to go beyond, and to out do.*

It's time to excel, to go beyond and to surpass. Don't settle for being average. Dare to be different. Go for the Gold and don't give up until you have attained it.

The Word says, *For whom the Lord loveth, he chasteneth* (Hebrews 12:6). **Chasteneth** means *corrects.* If you want to walk in God's best, then open yourself up to God for inspection and allow Him to reveal to you areas that need correction.

You Take the First Step

Draw nigh to God, and he will draw nigh to you. Cleanse your hands, ye sinners; and purify your hearts, ye double minded.

James 4:8

Notice the first part of that verse, *Draw nigh to God, and he will draw nigh to you.* What is God saying? "You take the first step. If you will take the first step toward Me, then you can count on it, I will come toward you." (Author's paraphrase).

It's up to us to take the initiative. We have an open invitation to enjoy close communion with God. How would you react if one of the most successful men of our generation sent you a letter inviting you to come and have dinner with him in his home? Would you accept the invitation? What if he said, "You can ask me anything you'd like to ask. I'll teach you everything I know about success."

You'd be foolish if you didn't accept his invitation. Well, that's what God is saying to you right now. Do you know anyone who knows more about success than He? He's saying, "I'm giving you an open invitation to draw nigh unto Me. And if you will, then I promise you this: I will draw nigh unto you."

God is telling us that we can be as close to Him as we desire to be.

No More Hiding

Notice it also says in that verse, *Cleanse your hands, ye sinners; and purify your hearts, ye double minded.* If you're going to get closer to God, then you're not going to be able to hide anything from Him. The closer you get to God, then the demand for a godly lifestyle intensifies.

Light Expels Darkness

As I said before, when Carolyn and I were dating, she insisted that we go to church.

One weekend, when I came home from college, she said, "We've got a revival going on at church!"

I thought, *Okay. If I'm going to see her, then I've got to go to a revival.*

The man who was preaching at that revival was William Branham. Her pastor and William Branham were very close friends, and Carolyn's great uncle, Young Brown, was William Branham's associate.

If you don't know anything about William Branham, he was a prophet of God and probably one of the most sensitive men to the Spirit of God that this generation has ever known, particularly in the area of the Word of Knowledge and the Discerning of Spirits.

Carolyn said, "There's a prophet at our church this week, and if you want to be with me, then you'll go to that meeting." I didn't even know what a prophet was.

The night before I went to that revival, I had been in the Fountain Blue Lounge where my buddies and I played pool, drank, and gambled from time to time. The next day, I got into my car and drove to Shreveport to be with Carolyn.

I drove to the church, and the place was packed out. There were hundreds of people standing around the building. I thought, *I'm not even going to be able to get in here. I won't even be able to see her.*

Then I noticed her standing at the door waiting for me. She had saved a seat for me.

Once they finished their singing, they introduced William Branham. I had never in my life been in a meeting like that before. When that man walked up to the platform, there was a presence about him that was different. The power of God fell in that place. And the more God manifested His power, the lower I got behind the pew in front of me.

He started calling people out of the audience stating what they'd been doing and where they had been. I kept sinking lower and lower in my seat. I just knew he was going to call me out. It scared me.

Carolyn said, "What's wrong with you?"

I said, "You don't want to know!"

I just knew he was going to call me out and reveal everything. People were falling on their faces repenting before God, getting baptized in the Holy Ghost, and I was wanting to get out of there. I was very uncomfortable. I was under conviction because I knew I was not living right. My parents didn't raise me that way. I knew I was living in sin. But I was not ready to change yet.

Carolyn's parents were the kind of people who always had the preacher at their house for dinner after the service. I usually had to go if I wanted to see Carolyn. Well, I excused myself that night. I was not going to that house if that *Prophet* was going to be there.

I will never forget that night when I drove back to college and walked into my apartment that I shared with three other guys. It had become a casino. I had never noticed it before, but suddenly, I saw darkness. I saw filth. I saw sin. I saw what I was living in, and I knew it wasn't right.

It was as if somebody turned the light on, and I could not believe what I had been living in. Even though I hadn't surrendered my life to God yet, I couldn't stand living there anymore. I packed up my things and moved out. I ended up renting a room from an elderly woman who had taken in college students for over 40 years. She was in her 80's, and she just loved to help young college kids.

She looked me straight in the eye and said, "I'm going to tell you something, son. I'd love to have you here, but there will be no drinking, no partying and no foul language here."

I knew that was what I needed. Suddenly, I began to realize that I was not only attracted to Carolyn, but I became attracted to what was in her and the commitment she had made to God.

The closer you get to God, the brighter His light will shine in your life and expel the darkness that's been there. God's not condemning you. He's not going to beat you over the head for the things you've been doing. But because He loves you, He will convict you so that you can correct those things and begin to experience His best for your life.

Don't Be Unequally Yoked

Be ye not unequally yoked together with unbelievers: for what fellowship hath righteousness with unrighteousness? and what communion hath light with darkness?

And what concord hath Christ with Belial? or what part hath he that believeth with an infidel?

And what agreement hath the temple of God with idols? for ye are the temple of the living God; as God hath said, I will dwell in them, and walk in them; and I will be their God, and they shall be my people.

*Wherefore **come out from among them,** and be ye separate, saith the Lord, and touch not the unclean thing; and I will receive you,*

And will be a Father unto you, and ye shall be my sons and daughters, saith the Lord Almighty.

2 Corinthians 6:14-18

Having therefore these promises, dearly beloved, let us cleanse ourselves from all filthiness of the flesh and spirit, perfecting holiness in the fear of God.

2 Corinthians 7:1

There may be some people or some influences in your life that you now know are no longer profitable. It doesn't take God speaking to you in a burning bush to reveal these things to you. The Holy Spirit has been dealing with you about these things, so why don't you go ahead and yield to Him.

The Bible is admonishing us to cleanse ourselves from all filthiness of the flesh and spirit. Once again, this demands that you take inventory of your life. It demands that you become willing to remove anything and everything that God considers to be filthiness.

Let me define for you the word *filthiness* from *W. E. Vine's Expository Dictionary* of Old and New Testament Words. *Filthiness* means *that which is characterized by moral impurity, defiling, disgraceful, and contrary to purity.* The word *purity* is defined as *uncontaminated.*

Are there things in your life that you know are contrary to purity? Then God is saying that it's time to clean up. Don't feel condemned, just put a stop to it right now.

Develop Godly Traits

If you're going for the Gold, then there are certain characteristics and qualities that you're going to have to start developing in your life.

One historian of past revivals and great moves of God stated that the kind of person God uses to initiate revival must possess the following characteristics:

1. Deep earnestness.

2. A desperate desire to see God move.

3. Unwavering faith.

4. Great patience.

5. A holy lifestyle.

6. A determination and a willingness to labor tirelessly.

7. Deep spirituality.

8. Nonconformity to the world.

9. Fervency in prayer.

Another church historian from the Welsh Revival of 1904 said that the following characteristics were present in those that God used in that great revival:

1. Total consecration and commitment.

2. Holiness.

3. An awareness of the majesty of God.

4. A deep spiritual life.

5. Utterly broken and remolded.

6. Surrendered and cleansed.

You'll notice the characteristics stated by two different historians were almost identical. In other words, these qualities are vital.

We must flee from all that contaminates and corrupts, and pursue righteousness and holy living. We must develop a greater thirst and a greater hunger for closer communion with God than we've ever experienced before. Consider the Holy Ghost as the Holy Guest in your home, in your car, at your workplace, and in everything you do. You'll find that as you practice His presence, then things that once held you back will fall away and become a thing of the past.

CHAPTER 4

How to Purge Yourself

4

How to Purge Yourself

In John 15:1-2 Jesus said, *I am the true vine, and my Father is the husbandman . . . every branch that beareth fruit, he purgeth it, that it may bring forth more fruit.*

In other words, if we are going to bear more fruit, then we have to go through a purging process.

Hebrews 4:12 says that the Word of God is a two-edged sword.   One side of that sword is for fighting the devil, but the other side is to be used as a spiritual surgical instrument for **you.** It is a purging instrument. There is a side of that sword that is designed by God to keep you clean. That's how we purge ourselves.

Spiritual Cleansing

But in a great house there are not only vessels of gold and of silver, but also of wood and of earth; and some to honour, and some to dishonour.

If a man therefore purge himself *from these, he shall be a vessel unto honour, sanctified, and meet for the master's use, and prepared unto every good work.*

Flee also youthful lusts: but follow righteousness, faith, charity, peace, with them that call on the Lord out of a pure heart.

2 Timothy 2:20-22

But in a great house there are not only vessels of gold and silver, but also [utensils] of wood and earthenware, and some for honorable and noble [use] and some for menial and ignoble [use].

So whoever cleanses himself *[from what is ignoble and unclean, who separates himself from contact with contaminating and corrupting influ-*

ences] will [then himself] be a vessel set apart and useful for honorable and noble purposes, consecrated and profitable to the Master, fit and ready for any good work.

Shun youthful lusts and flee from them, and aim at and pursue righteousness (all that is virtuous and good, right living, conformity to the will of God in thought, word, and deed); [and aim at and pursue] faith, love, [and] peace (harmony and concord with others) in fellowship with all [Christians], who call upon the Lord out of a pure heart.

2 Timothy 2:20-22 (Amplified)

If you want to be a vessel of honor, then there are certain things that you're going to be required to do.

When I began studying these things and praying over them, I decided to go through my house and make sure I didn't have anything that would be considered defiling, morally impure, disgraceful, or contrary to a holy life. I went through every closet and every drawer.

Somebody might say, "Brother Jerry, aren't you getting a little picky?"

Yes, but only because I'm hungry for God. I'm hungry for a greater anointing. I want God's best, and I'm going for the Gold.

You might say, "Brother Jerry, this sounds too hard. How could I ever live up to these standards?"

First, you've got to want God's best more than anything else. It's not a hard standard to live up to when you want it more than anything else in your life.

In Philippians 3:10-11, the Apostle Paul says, *That I may know him, and the power of his resurrection, and the fellowship of his sufferings, being made conformable unto his death;*

If by any means I might attain unto the resurrection of the dead.

The Amplified Bible says, *[For my determined purpose is] that I may know Him [that I may pro-*

gressively become more deeply and intimately acquainted with Him . . .

What a powerful statement! Paul said that knowing Him was his determined purpose. It's got to become your determined purpose to experience God's best, or it will never happen in your life.

There is too much at stake to keep permitting unprofitable things in our lives anymore. We simply can't allow anything in our lives that would hinder us from having God's best.

Steps to Purging Yourself:

1. <u>You Make the Choice</u>

The Bible says, *If a man therefore purge himself . . .* so again this purging process is something you're going to have to initiate. It's going to be something that you do as an act of your own will. It is your choice. Why? Because you want to be a vessel of honor.

Notice it doesn't say, "God will purge you." No, you purge yourself. God will reveal to you what needs purging, but you're the one who has to do the purging.

If is a conditional word. In other words, the choice is yours. You can be a vessel of honor or a vessel of dishonor. You are the one who determines this.

If a man therefore purge himself from these, he shall be a vessel unto honour, sanctified . . . The word **sanctified** just simply means *separated or set apart.* God wants to separate you. Why? Because He wants His power flowing through you unhindered. He wants to use you mightily in these last days for His glory.

So whoever cleanses himself [from what is ignoble and unclean, who separates himself from contact with contaminating and corrupting influences] will [then himself] be a vessel set apart and useful for honorable and noble purposes, consecrated and profitable to the Master, fit and ready for any good work.

2 Timothy 2:21 (Amplified)

God wants to be able to hold us up as a trophy and say, "Here is one that I can and will use mightily . . . here is a vessel of honor."

2. <u>Yield to the Holy Spirit</u>

As I've mentioned before, the Holy Spirit is the One who will show you the unprofitable things in your life. However, once He reveals them, then you must be willing to obey Him and remove them immediately. He will not only show you what needs to be corrected, but He will also assist you in purging yourself so that you will become more fruitful.

Condemnation vs. Conviction

The Body of Christ has been confused about the difference between condemnation and conviction. Many think that they're one and the same.

Condemnation comes from Satan. Condemnation does not provide a way out. It does not give a solution to the problem. It just continually beats you over the head and tells you what a failure you are. *Conviction* is from the Holy Ghost, and it always provides a way out. It produces freedom.

If you yield to the Holy Spirit's conviction, then it will produce repentance, correction, and then maturity. There is no condemnation to them that are in Christ Jesus, who walk after the Spirit and not the flesh (Romans 8:1).

When I was pastoring a church many years ago, as long as I was preaching prosperity, blessing, healing and success, everybody loved me. But the moment I began talking about commitment, consecration and holiness, some of them started backstroking out of the church.

I'm not trying to condemn anybody by sharing these important truths. I am trying to get us to face some facts. It's time to make sure our lives are pure and stop playing religious games.

3. <u>Change Your Way of Living</u>

Flee also youthful lusts: but follow righteousness, faith, charity, peace, with them that call on the Lord out of a pure heart.

2 Timothy 2:22

Shun youthful lusts and flee from them, and aim at and pursue righteousness (all that is virtuous and good, right living, conformity to the will of God in thought, word, and deed); [and aim at and pursue] faith, love, [and] peace (harmony and concord with others) in fellowship with all [Christians], who call upon the Lord out of a pure heart.

2 Timothy 2:22 (Amplified)

The Amplified Bible defines **pursuing right-eousness** as this: *all that is virtuous and good, right living, conformity to the will of God in thought, in word, and in deed.*

Again, if you're going to be a vessel of honor, you've got to become more aware of your actions, your conversation, the things you have contact with, the places you go, the people you're around, the things you read, and the things you watch.

4. <u>Don't Accept What the World Accepts</u>

We live in a world that is getting darker and darker. How do you and I live in this world without being contaminated? It's going to take some discipline on our part, or we'll not be able to do it.

I'm not saying, "Thou shalt not ever watch television again." I am saying to be selective about what you watch.

The world has tried to desensitize us by using different terminology to describe sin. They gradually sneak more and more perversion into prime time television programs to cause us to become accustomed to it. Without even realizing it, your favorite television program could be something that grieves the Holy Spirit.

When you have become desensitized, then perversion becomes tolerable. What's happening? Satan is conditioning us to accept what the world accepts.

I'm not saying that if you're going to be used mightily of God you can never watch television again. That's not what I'm saying at all. Once again, what I'm saying is, "Be selective." Make sure the Holy Ghost is comfortable with everything you're participating in.

5. <u>Shun the Very Appearance of Evil</u>

Everything is permissible (allowable and lawful) for me; but not all things are helpful (good for me to do, expedient and profitable when considered with other things). Everything is lawful for me, but I will not become the slave of anything or be brought under its power.

1 Corinthians 6:12 (Amplified)

Notice the Amplified says that all things are *permissible and allowable,* but not all things are *helpful, good for me to do, expedient and profitable.* As I said before, if you're going to obtain the Gold, then you're going to have to allow God to reveal to you the unprofitable things. Then you have to be willing to give them up or be willing to remove them.

For instance, I love sports. I am a sports enthusiast, and my favorite sport is boxing. I love boxing with a passion. I can't watch a boxing match without helping them fight. When the fight is over, I am absolutely worn out; I need a rub down and a shower. I really get into it.

Several years ago, I had the privilege of discipling a professional boxer in the Word. After fighting professionally for a while, he retired and then went to work for one of the boxing promoters. From time to time, he would call me or send me a note and say, "Would you like to come to this championship fight? I've got a ring-side seat for you."

If you know anything about a ring-side seat at one of these major championship fights, it costs anywhere from $1,000 to $2,500 depending on how big the fight is. So, for a person who loves boxing, to be given a ring-side seat — that's got to be God!

So, I went to see this big fight. And guess where it was held? Caesar's Palace, Las Vegas, Nevada! Now, I wasn't going there to gamble. I wasn't going there to sin. I don't drink; I don't gamble; I don't run around. I was going to Las Vegas to watch a fight. It was totally permissible. It was allowable. It isn't unlawful. And it was a desire of my heart.

But it was where the fight was held that bothered me. I had to stay at Caesar's Palace. You can't get to the elevator to get to your room without going through the casino. They designed it that way on purpose so that people will be attracted to the gambling tables.

I had no intentions of gambling. I simply wanted to watch a championship fight.

So I was walking through the casino to get to the elevator, and I was thinking to myself, *Oh God, I hope nobody sees me in here! What if somebody sees me?*

I kept thinking about what an old Apostle of God told me years before. He said, "Now, Jerry, I'm going to give you some advice that will help you. Listen to me and adhere to this, and you'll be a success."

I thought, *Man! He's going to give me a powerful key!*

You know what his key was? **"Shun the very appearance of evil."** There I was walking through the casino thinking of those words, and suddenly, I heard, "Hey! Brother Jerry!"

I thought, *O Dear God! Somebody has recognized me. I'm not turning around.*

Again I heard, "Hey! Brother Jerry!"

I turned around, and it was a card dealer at one of the tables.

He yelled, "I watch you on TV all the time! I've just gotten saved and I'm believing for another job."

Then he asked the people at the table, "How many cards do you want?"

I kept hearing in my spirit, "Shun the very appearance of evil. Shun the very appearance of evil."

I wasn't doing anything evil; I was simply going to a fight! But how could I prove to this new believer that I really wasn't there to gamble, or to cheat on my wife, or to drink alcohol? I was really there to watch a fight. I was innocent. It was the appearance of evil that bothered me.

I went to my room, and I was miserable. I was supposed to be happy. I had a ring-side seat waiting for me. I didn't have to pay for it. It was given to me.

So, now it's time for the fight, and I had to walk through the casino again. They had set up a special arena in the parking lot because there were 25,000 people attending the fight that night, and they couldn't fit them all in the indoor arena.

I walked in and found my seat, and boy, was it a good seat! It turned out that I was sitting right behind Mohammed Ali.

Now, prior to going to the fight, I called my friend, Pastor Ray McCauley from South Africa, and told him that I was going. Ray likes boxing too, so he had several guys from his church come to his house so they could watch the fight on television, and they would look for me in the crowd.

So, as it turned out, I sat right behind Mohammed Ali. Right before the fight started, the TV cameras began closing in on Mohammed Ali. So, I just leaned to the side of him and waved and said, "Hey, Ray!"

Later, Ray told me that all the guys at his house saw me and started jumping up yelling, "There's Jerry! There's Jerry!"

It never crossed my mind that not only did Ray McCauley see me, but 900 million other people around the world saw Jerry Savelle at Caesar's Palace in Las Vegas as well.

Later, I wondered how many of my partners might have been sitting in their homes watching that fight and said, "Wasn't that Jerry Savelle! What's he doing there?"

I was innocent. It was permissible; it was allowable. I wasn't sinning. I was just watching the fight. However, my being there could have been a stumbling block for someone else.

Not long after that, I received another invitation to attend a championship fight with a ringside seat. It was Sugar Ray Leonard vs. Roberto Duran. Wow! I was a Sugar Ray Leonard fan. I could hardly wait.

This time, the fight was held in New Orleans, Louisiana! I went and once again I had a great seat.

Soon a gentleman sat next to me on the right. Then, another guy sat on my left side. I've never seen them before, and there I was in the middle of these two strangers.

In a little while, one leaned over to talk to the other one and said, "I'll bet you $10,000 that Duran's going to win."

The other one said, "I'll bet you $15,000 Sugar Ray will win."

I was just sitting there minding my own business but they're both leaning over me to make their bets. I couldn't help but hear their conversation.

One of them said, "$15,000? Why don't you make it $20,000?"

Then the other one said, "Put your money where your mouth is! Let's go $25,000."

He said, "All right. $25,000."

I was sitting there thinking, *Twenty-five thousand dollars?*

In a little while, one of them said, "Well, who's going to hold the money?"

Then they both looked at me and said, "What do you do?"

I said, "I'm a preacher."

They said, "A preacher? What are you doing here?"

I said, "I like the fights. I'm here for the fight."

One of them said, "I've never met a preacher at the fights before."

I said, "Well, I'm a preacher who likes the fights."

He said, "All right. We can trust the preacher. Give him the money."

The next thing I knew, they both put $25,000 in my coat pocket. That's when I heard in my spirit, "Shun the very appearance of evil! Shun the very appearance of evil."

I thought, *I'm innocent! I'm not doing anything wrong!*

But it doesn't look that way! What if somebody in the stands, looking down at ring-side, recognized me and saw money going into Jerry Savelle's pockets?

I would have never been able to explain to them what happened. That's how rumors get started.

"We saw Jerry Savelle taking money in the Super Dome!"

How would I have ever been able to explain that?

Finally, I got a revelation: I don't belong in places like that. As much as I enjoy boxing, I can no longer be seen in a place like that. I just can't go there. It's unprofitable for me.

I'm not saying that it's wrong for anyone else. I'm just sharing with you one of the things that I had to be willing to remove from my life because of who I am and my responsibility in the Body of Christ.

I can still watch boxing on television, but I no longer go to where they're taking place. It's unprofitable for me to be in that environment.

6. <u>Be Aggressive</u>

If you're going for the Gold, then you're going to have to be aggressive. You can't be passive about the unprofitable things in your life. You have to aggressively flee from them. And you must aggresively pursue righteousness.

The Amplified defines **righteousness** as *all that is virtuous, good, right living, and all that is in conformity to the will of God in thought, in word, and in deed.*

Flee One and Pursue Another

We need to flee lust and things that corrupt, and aggressively pursue right living, moral living, and things that we know are pleasing to God.

Flee anything that will contaminate or corrupt, and pursue everything that has to do with right living. Being passive about things that contaminate and corrupt will not make you a vessel of honor. You have to ask yourself, "How desperate am I to be used mightily by God?"

That ye may be blameless and harmless, the sons of God, without rebuke, in the midst of a crooked and perverse nation, among whom ye shine as lights in the world.

Philippians 2:15

The Amplified Bible says, *That you may show yourselves to be blameless and guileless, innocent and uncontaminated, children of God without blemish (faultless, unrebukable) in the midst of a crooked and wicked generation [spiritually perverted and perverse], among whom you are seen as bright lights (stars or beacons shining out clearly) in the [dark] world.*

Take an aggressive stand against sin and all moral impurity. And at the same time, be just as aggressive in pursuing holiness.

7. <u>Dare to be Different</u>

God realizes that the world we live in is perverted, contaminated, and corrupted, but He wants us to stand out in the crowd. That was the message of Jesus in all of His teachings: Dare to be different.

God's not going to ask us to do something that we cannot do. If He asks us to do it, then He will also supply the ability and the power to get the job done. That's why He sent the Holy Ghost. He's our helper.

How Desperate Are You?

I believe with all my heart that from here on out, it's not just what we preach that will impact people, but it is also how people see us conduct our everyday lives. People are fed up with Christians who preach one thing and live another. God wants to use your life as a soul-winning tool. So demand from yourself that you are going to live a holy lifestyle.

CHAPTER 5

Don't Lose Your Focus

5

Don't Lose Your Focus

I'm endeavoring to be just as open and honest with you as I possibly can. I never preach something that I'm not already appropriating in my own life. Please continue to read this book with an open mind and a teachable spirit.

Rearrange Your Priorities

[For my determined purpose is] that I may know Him [that I may progressively become more deeply and intimately acquainted with Him . . .

Philippians 3:10 (Amplified)

I would interpret that as Paul saying that his priority in life was to know God. As well as he already knew God, he wanted a deeper, intimate relationship with Him. He wanted to be in His perfect will, live a life that was pleasing to Him and be an instrument for His glory.

How do you make a closer relationship with God a priority in your life?

And there is none that calleth upon thy name, that stirreth up himself to take hold of thee: for thou hast hid thy face from us, and hast consumed us, because of our iniquities.

Isaiah 64:7

Notice the phrase **stirreth up.** *W. E. Vine's Expository Dictionary* defines **stirreth up** as *to kindle afresh, to keep in full flame.* *W. E. Vine's* also says that the phrase, **stirreth up,** is used metaphorically as *a fire that is capable of dying out because of neglect.*

Would you say that your relationship with God has dwindled away because of neglect? Has your prayer time been reduced to Sunday mornings and just before meal time? It could be that you just need to rekindle your relationship with Him. How do you do that?

Divided Interests

Let's read James 4:8 once again: *Draw nigh to God, and he will draw nigh to you. Cleanse your hands, ye sinners; and purify your hearts, **ye double minded**.*

The Amplified says it this way . . . **_wavering individuals with divided interests_** . . .

That is how the flame goes out. When you have divided interests, you can neglect your time with God.

When the things of this world become more important than an intimate relationship with God, then we have divided interests. When believing God for prosperity becomes more important than an intimate relationship with God, then that's divided interests.

Years ago, the Lord said this to me:

"Stop seeking the provisions; start seeking the Provider. If you seek the Provider, provisions come with Him."

What is God saying?

"Develop an intimate relationship with Me, and then everything I have is yours." (Author's paraphrase).

The Lord also said to me, "I said in My Word, 'Seek My face.' My people are seeking My hands. My hands represent provision; My face represents intimacy." When you have intimacy with God, then you will also have His provisions.

Those of you who are parents: How would you like it if the only time your children ever came into your presence to talk to you was when they had a need? That's not relationship.

That's the way most of God's people are. The only time they ever want to visit with Him is when they have a need. God is saying to us that if we will develop an intimate relationship with Him, then He will bless us with everything He has. He will give us anything we need.

Knowing God must become the most important thing in our lives. He has to be priority if we want to attain the Gold.

Don't Allow Hobbies to be Distractions

Sometimes, if we aren't careful, we can allow our hobbies to become a divided interest. There's nothing wrong with having hobbies, but be sure that they never cause you to neglect your time with God.

In my own life, I realized that some of my hobbies were taking too much of my time. I had to rearrange my priorities.

For example, I thoroughly enjoy riding motorcycles. I have a passion for it. But I remember when I allowed that love and passion to cross the line. It was becoming too much of a priority in my life. Only you can determine when you've crossed that line. It's not my job to judge you. I'm judging myself, and I know when I cross the line.

One time, I jumped on my brand new Harley Davidson that had less than 500 miles on it and took off! The entire time I was riding that day, somehow I knew I had crossed the line. I realized that I had allowed this hobby to consume me. Suddenly, I realized, "I am now riding somebody else's motorcycle. This is not mine anymore."

I knew that I needed to make some changes in my life and rearrange my priorities . . . if I wanted God's best.

God didn't say, "Get rid of it," but on the inside, I knew I needed to give it up.

I rode home, pulled it up in the garage and said, "Lord, You tell me who You want me to give it to, and it's out of here." And He did, instantly.

I had another one, so I said, "What about this one?"

He said, "That's up to you."

I said, "Well, then, I'm giving them both away."

So I did. And you know what? I didn't cry

when they left. I didn't say, "Oh God! I wish I hadn't given them away!"

No! There was a freedom that came. I showed God that He is first place in my life. God never told me that I had to do that, but I just knew in my spirit that I needed to. And I didn't even miss them when they were gone.

About a year later, my oldest grandson, Mark James, who has been riding motorcycles with me ever since he was big enough to walk, said to me, "PaPa, is Jesus going to give us another Harley?"

I said, "Well, son, I don't know. I haven't asked Him for one."

He said, "PaPa, didn't you give yours away?"

I said, "Yes."

He said, "Haven't you taught me that if you give you receive?"

I said, "Yes."

He said, "Then why wouldn't Jesus give you another one?"

I said, "I haven't asked Him. Have you?"

He said, "Yes!"

I said, "What did Jesus say to you?"

I'll never forget what he said. He looked at me and said, "PaPa, I think Jesus is just like you."

I said, "What do you mean by that?"

He said, "He's thinking about it!"

I said, "What do you mean, 'He's thinking about it'?"

He said, "I asked Jesus to give my PaPa another motorcycle so we could ride, and He's thinking about it just like you do sometimes. Sometimes I'll ask you if I can have something, and you'll just give it to me. Then other times you say, 'I'll think about it.'"

I said, "What happens when I tell you that I'll think about it?"

A big smile came to his face and he said, "I get it!"

Well, I found out that Jesus was thinking about it, and I wound up with more motorcycles. I enjoy them now, but they don't control me. In fact, we've turned our motorcycle riding into a ministry and an outreach, and now we're winning people to Jesus through them.

Owning a motorcycle is not a sin. Playing golf is not a sin. Hobbies, sports and recreation are not sinful. God is not saying that you cannot participate in sports or have hobbies. He is saying don't allow them to cause you to neglect your time with Him. In other words, keep them in their place. Enjoy them, have fun with them, but if you ever notice that they're causing you to spend less time with God, then do whatever you need to do to take control.

Avoid Distractions

And the cares of this world, and the deceitfulness of riches, and the lusts of other things entering in, choke the word, and it becometh unfruitful.

Mark 4:19

The Amplified Bible says it this way: *Then the cares and anxieties of the world and distractions of the age, and the pleasure and delight and false glamour and deceitfulness of riches, and the craving and passionate desire for other things creep in and choke and suffocate the Word, and it becomes fruitless.*

Nobody ever wakes up one morning and says, "I think I'll be distracted today." It doesn't happen that way.

Distractions come when you fail to spend time with God.

If you don't keep yourself stirred up, then you can be easily distracted by the things of this world.

I discovered that the phrase ***stir up*** also implies *to shake yourself, to urge yourself, and to incite yourself to action.*

I mentioned previously that *W. E. Vine's* defines **stir up** as *to kindle afresh, or to keep in full flame.* How do we do this?

O God, thou art my God; early will I seek thee: my soul thirsteth for thee, my flesh longeth for thee in a dry and thirsty land, where no water is; To see thy power and thy glory . . .

Psalm 63:1-2

You have to ask yourself, "What am I willing to do to see God's power and God's glory? How important is this in my life?"

Don't Look Back

When I was in high school, I was very involved in sports. Once, while participating in a track and field event, I was scheduled to run the one mile race. I was in great shape; I was focused; and I just knew that I was going to win the race.

The gun sounded and we took off. I was running well, and I was in the lead. In fact, I was so far in the lead that I wondered just how far ahead of my opponents I was. So, I turned my head back to see where they were, and suddenly, I lost my footing, tripped, fell down and they passed me by.

The moral of that story is: **never look back.** It could cost you the race. Everything you want, need or desire is ahead of you, not behind you.

If you've made the decision to go for the Gold and to believe for God's best in every area of your life, then you've got to stay focused. There can be no turning back in your life. Don't look at the things you gave up to go for the Gold. Those things are nothing in comparison to attaining the Gold.

When you look back, you lose your focus. You need to keep your eyes on Jesus, and He will give you the ability to win your race. When you look back, you are admitting that you're not ready to give up your former way of living. You've got to release the past and keep your eyes on the finish line.

Don't Waste Your Potential

Years ago, I was able to sit down on a Sunday afternoon and watch the Super Bowl. It was the Pittsburgh Stealers and the Dallas Cowboys playing for the championship.

I was just sitting there having a good time watching these guys play football, and suddenly I heard the Holy Ghost speak to me.

He said, "How many Roger Staubacks, Drew Pearsons, Terry Bradshaws, and Frank O'Harrisses do you suppose are sitting in front of their television sets today watching these men play?"

I said, "Say that again."

He said, "How many Roger Staubacks, Drew Pearsons, Terry Bradshaws, and Frank O'Harrisses do you suppose are sitting in front of their television sets today watching these men play?"

Suddenly I understood what He was saying.

He said, "Son, there are many men who have the same potential as those athletes, but the difference is, those men are in the game; the others are just talking about what they *could have* been."

What's the difference? Some tap their potential and some don't. Discipline, commitment, and focus are the difference.

There have been many professional athletes who have wasted their potential. They did not restrict themselves in all things. They had great potential, but they lost their focus. It's the same in the Body of Christ. There's a lot of wasted potential. There are many believers who have lost their focus.

There have been many preachers who were eloquent, intelligent, charismatic and appeared to have it all together, and yet I hear about them committing adultery or stealing the money and immediately I think, "wasted potential." They lost their focus.

You and I have the potential to be Gold Medallists in the kingdom of God . . . but we're going to have to stay focused just like that athlete who trains year after year for the Olympics. He sets his sights for attaining the Gold, and he refuses to allow anything to distract him.

I press toward the mark for the prize of the high calling of God in Christ Jesus.

Philippians 3:14

Anyone who is going for the Gold cannot allow nor afford distractions.

One of the things that I admire about great athletes is not only the physical training that they go through, but the mental training as well. They are focused.

Looking unto Jesus the author and finisher of our faith . . .

Hebrews 12:2

In other words, we look to Him as our example. He is the One we are to stay focused on. Don't take your eyes off of Jesus.

The Amplified says it this way, *Looking away [from all that will distract] to Jesus.*

Purpose today that you will remain focused. Don't ever lose your determination for achieving maximum results in every area of your life.

CHAPTER 6

*Your Training
Starts Now*

6

Your Training Starts Now

You've absorbed a great deal of information, and now you are ready to begin your training. God is demanding that we get into spiritual shape. He is calling us to a holy lifestyle. Let's not disappoint Him. If we are willing to obey, then there's nothing the devil can do that can keep us from being blessed.

Blessed is the Man That . . .

As part of your training, I encourage you to become familiar with the following Scriptures. You will discover right away that there are many rewards for living a life of holiness.

1. Psalm 1:1-2 – *Blessed is the man that **walketh not in the counsel of the ungodly, nor standeth in the way of sinners, nor sitteth in the seat of the scornful.***

But his delight is in the law of the Lord; and in his law doth he meditate day and night.

2. Psalm 32:1-2 (Amplified) – *Blessed (happy, fortunate, to be envied) is he who* **has forgiveness of his transgression continually exercised upon him, whose sin is covered.**

Blessed (happy, fortunate, to be envied) is the man to whom **the Lord imputes no iniquity and in whose spirit there is no deceit.**

3. Psalm 40:4 (Amplified) – *Blessed (happy, fortunate, to be envied) is the man who* **makes the Lord his refuge and trust, and turns not to the proud or to followers of false gods.**

4. Psalm 65:4 (Amplified) – *Blessed (happy, fortunate, to be envied) is the man whom* **You choose and cause to come near, that he may dwell in Your courts!**

Those who practice the presence of God are going to be blessed.

5. Psalm 84:4 – *Blessed are they that **dwell in thy house:** they will be still praising thee.*

6. Psalm 94:12 (Amplified) – *Blessed (happy, fortunate, to be envied) is the man whom **You discipline and instruct, O Lord, and teach out of Your law.***

The King James says, *Blessed is the man whom thou chastenest.*

In other words, God is saying if you want to be blessed, keep yourself open for correction and instruction.

7. Psalm 106:3 (Amplified) – *Blessed (happy, fortunate, to be envied) are **those who observe justice [treating others fairly] and who do right and are in right standing with God at all times.***

8. Psalm 112:1 – *Blessed is the man **that feareth the Lord, that delighteth greatly in his commandments.***

9. Revelation 1:3 – *Blessed is he that **readeth . . . and keep those things which are written therein.***

129

You are now aware of God's expectations of you before the appearing of Jesus. His return is so close and there is much to be done. We don't want anything holding us back. We've got to remove every distraction, stay focused and keep our eyes on Jesus.

I encourage you to read every chapter in this book until this becomes a revelation to you. Just hearing it or reading it one time is probably not enough. Holiness and walking in the fear of the Lord has to become a lifestyle. It can't just be something you try. Trying won't produce the Gold. You have to go for it with everything that is in you—and never look back.

Remember, walking in the fear of the Lord is nothing more than loving what God loves and hating what God hates. Think about this in every decision you make.

You have what it takes to win the Gold. You're in training, your mind is being renewed, you're developing discipline, and God is going to reward you with His best. You are a part of the *Last*

Frontier before the appearing of Jesus. Don't settle for anything less than God's best.

ABOUT THE AUTHOR

Dr. Jerry Savelle is a noted author, evangelist, and teacher who travels extensively throughout the United States, Canada, and around the globe. He is president of Jerry Savelle Ministries International, a ministry of many outreaches devoted to meeting the needs of believers all over the world.

Well-known for his balanced Biblical teaching, Dr. Savelle has conducted seminars, crusades and conventions for over thirty years as well as ministered in thousands of churches and fellowships. He is in great demand today because of his inspiring message of victory and faith and his vivid, and often humorous, illustrations from the Bible. He teaches the uncompromised Word of God with a power and an authority that is exciting, but with a love that delivers the message directly to the spirit man.

In addition to his international headquarters in Crowley, Texas, Dr. Savelle is also founder of JSMI-Kenya; JSMI-United Kingdom; JSMI-South Africa; JSMI-Tanzania; JSMI-Australia; and JSMI-Asia.

He is also founder and President of JSMI Bible Institute and School of World Evangelism in the USA, Kenya, the United Kingdom and Micronesia. It is a two-year school for the preparation of ministers to take the Gospel of Jesus Christ to the nations of the world.

In addition, the missions outreach of his ministry extends to over 50 countries around the world.

Dr. Savelle has authored many books and has an extensive video and cassette teaching tape ministry and a worldwide television broadcast. Thousands of books, tapes, and videos are distributed around the world each year through Jerry Savelle Ministries International.

For a complete list of tapes, videos and books by Jerry Savelle, write or call:

Jerry Savelle Ministries International
P. O. Box 748
Crowley, TX 76036
817/297-3155

Feel free to include your prayer requests and comments when you write.
Visit us at our website:
www.jsmi.org

OTHER BOOKS BY JERRY SAVELLE:

FOR THOSE WHO DON'T KNOW JESUS, WOULD YOU LIKE TO KNOW HIM?

If you were to die today, where would you spend eternity? If you have accepted Jesus Christ as your personal Lord and Savior, you can be assured that when you die, you will go directly into the presence of God in Heaven. If you have not accepted Jesus as your personal Lord and Savior, is there any reason why you can't make Jesus the Lord of your life right now? Please pray this prayer out loud, and as you do, pray with a sincere and trusting heart, and you will be born again.

DEAR GOD IN HEAVEN,

I come to You in the Name of Jesus to receive salvation and eternal life. I believe that Jesus is Your Son. I believe that He died on the cross for my sins, and that You raised Him from the dead. I receive Jesus now into my heart and make Him the Lord of my life. Jesus, come into my heart. I welcome You as my Lord and Savior. Father, I believe Your Word that says I am now saved. I confess with my mouth that I am saved and born again. I am now a child of God.